YOUR KNOWLEDGE HAS VALUE

Ayse Gökce

Khaled Hosseini: "A Thousand Splendid Suns"

GRIN Verlag

Bibliografische Information der Deutschen Nationalbibliothek:

Die Deutsche Bibliothek verzeichnet diese Publikation in der Deutschen National-
bibliografie; detaillierte bibliografische Daten sind im Internet über http://dnb.d-
nb.de/ abrufbar.

Imprint:

Copyright © 2011 GRIN Verlag GmbH
Druck und Bindung: Books on Demand GmbH, Norderstedt Germany
ISBN: 978-3-640-90867-7

Friedrich-Alexander-Universität Erlangen-Nürnberg

Lehrstuhl für Fremdsprachendidaktik mit Schwerpunkt Didaktik des Englischen
5. Fachsemester

Seminar "Young Adult Fiction"

Seminararbeit am Lehrstuhl Fremdsprachendidaktik

Khaled Hosseini: *A Thousand Splendid Suns*

vorgelegt von:
Ayse Gökce

28.02.2011 (09.03.2011)

Contents

1   Introduction

Teaching English as a foreign language means a great challenge which would certainly be answered by all English teachers in the affirmative. Today every school in Germany offers English as school subject, even the primary schools. Consequently it must be put great emphasis on teaching it accurately by taking into consideration any aspect of English language acquisition when learning it, for example the acquisition of a distinctive vocabulary, the ability to use grammar rules correctly, the ability to spell correctly, the ability to understand what is been said when native speakers talk in English which we call listening comprehension. Another very important part of learning English as a foreign language is undisputedly reading comprehension. The ability to read out correctly, to understand what is been read and to be able to work with a text effectively is not only a competence that should be concentrated on in the foreign language but also in the mother tongue. The PISA Study is a perfect proof of this which will be mentioned later on. In this paper I will try to accentuate the importance and significance of reading in the English class. In order to illustrate this I will introduce the novel *A Thousand Splendid Suns* by Khaled Hosseini, an American author and doctor with Afghan origins, and use it for the elaboration of the importance of reading activities in the English class. Initially I will focus on the didactic analysis which includes the reference to the syllabus. The syllabus is of course the signpost in terms of guidelines when planning the lessons, choosing age-appropriate media and methods. What role does reading play in this context? What is said in the syllabus when it comes to reading? The next step would be to explain why I have chosen *A Thousand Splendid Suns* in this context. For what reason I am of the opinion that it can be read in the grade and school given below. I also focus on the topics that can be made use of in class when working with the novel, which aspects given in the text could be used to discuss it with pupils. Then the novel will be summarized in short by also taking into account the author's vita in short to have a better understanding of what is important in the usage of the book. After this didactic analysis there will also be a methodical analysis which includes a portrayal of the procedure which means this contains information about which school and which grade should consult this novel in class. Also important is here the duration of the text work and the alternation of tasks to avoid monotony which will be explained later on in chapter 3.1. This portrayal is followed by the lesson plan which is worked out for twelve lessons. One of the lessons, namely the second lesson is explained in detail in tabular form which also informs about the time that is given to each step during the lesson. The résumé focuses on the point whether this novel is appropriate for the given

class or not and the reasons for this. In the conclusion there will be a personal opinion on the question in how far this novel is highly recommended for reading comprehension in the English class and if so, which conditions must be there to use this text accurately. Moreover the importance of reading in school per se is mentioned to point out whether it is essential or not.

2. Didactic Analysis

2.1 Reference to Syllabus

Why reading in the English class? What is the importance of reading texts in the foreign language? "Reading is like an infectious disease: it is caught not taught. And you can't catch it from someone who hasn't got it himself"[1] This quotation refers to the fact that the motivation to read is an essential premise to develop a reading competence. In this context the foreign language class should contribute to the establishment of an age-appropriate reading culture. So as I mentioned beforehand the enhancement of reading in the English class is undisputedly an enrichment in terms of establishing foreign language skills but it also stimulates reading in general, for example in the mother tongue. Statistics prove that there is a massive lack of reading motivation in the case of children. The PISA Study, for example, found out in 2001 that many children hardly read or do not read at all. 42 % of them do not read because of the pleasure to be experienced and 31% are of the opinion that reading means a waste of time. Interestingly enough, 55% of the boys are nonreaders. The interest to read diminishes intensely: This is given for children aged 8 to 10 and those between 11 and 13 years of age. So what the school has to do here is to convey basic reading experiences. Hurrelmann (2003) says that pupils rarely read in class in order to gain emotional benefit and aesthetic pleasure. Texts used in class should be age-appropriate respectively appropriate for the pupils, the topics should be interesting for teenagers, for example they should include aspects like the transition to adulthood, the search of one's identity, problems with parents, teachers and peers. They should not overcharge in a linguistic manner, the difficulty level should also be appropriate. Authenticity is also essential so that the pupils can better understand what the text says. And they should get

[1] Cf. Fässler, Georg: Aufbaukurs Lektüre: *Reading*. Wintersemester 2010/11. Uni Erlangen-Nürnberg

the opportunity to be included in terms of choosing literature in the class. Furthermore the text should allow various kinds of motivational methods for textual work.[2] In terms of

reading comprehension the Bavarian syllabus for the tenth grade Realschule emphasizes that it is the aim of the English class for pupils to be able to deduce long and unknown texts on their own and to interpret them. They shall be able to perceive the author's intention, the genre of the text and the structure of the text referring to the content. It is important that the pupils understand authentic texts with few unknown language elements. The tenth grade requires topics like aspects of society, culture and science deriving from the English speaking world. In preparation for language acquaintances that take place extracurricular, authentic listening and reading texts play a great role in this grade. In this context it is vital that texts are included that enhance the person to utter statements or enable the exchange of ideas. As far as reading comprehension is concerned it is the aim of the English class at Realschule that pupils get the ability to interpret authentic material for projects and presentations independently, for example in the Internet. They learn how to read simple literary texts among others autonomously and to compare topics in various papers, for example quality press and popular press.[3] The syllabus of Hesse for the tenth grade Realschule says – to name another German syllabus – that reading skills are essential for the following tasks: a pupil should be able to isolate a text thematically by its title and by using his or her foreknowledge. This knowledge should then be used to classify the texts. Moreover reading should be put emphasis on so that the children can filter out the essence of a text, and recognize the main problem that is portrayed in it.[4] So it can be concluded that reading in the English class is indispensable and an essential part of foreign language acquisition as well as the acquisition of vital skill in terms of textual work both in English and in another language.

2.2   Purpose of Lesson Plan

The decision to chose this novel is evident. It is relatively new as it was first published in Great Britain in 2007. Usually students tend to prefer books that are not that old of date. Moreover the first novel of the author Khaled Hosseini, The Kite Runner, gained

---

[2]Cf. Fässler, Georg. Ibd.
[3]http://www.isb.bayern.de/isb/download.aspx?DownloadFileID=51433e746908a327e2b5df4a1ecfe326
   (6.03.2011)
[4]http://download.bildung.hessen.de/unterricht/lernarchiv/lehrplaene/realschule/englisch/LPRealEnglisch.p
   df (6.03.2011)

so much recognition that it is obvious that this book will be interesting for students, too, as far as the latter know the first novel for it is important to also take the students into consideration when choosing a book to work on in class. For Realschule I would recommend it for the tenth grade but not earlier as the topics in the novel require a certain maturity because of

topics such as domestic violence, the position of women in society and social isolation among other things. Furthermore the vocabulary given in the book is better suited for students older than 15 years as they have a greater vocabulary and possess more knowledge about the foreign language than their younger school friends. *A Thousand Splendid Suns* offers a wide range of topics pupils can effectively work on. First of all it draws a colorful picture of Afghanistan in general as a foreign country, culture and nation but also the Afghanistan as it was like before the Russian Invasion and the later reign by the Taliban and last but not least the post-Afghanistan with all the violence and war it has to face today. Some of the facts and issues that are mentioned in the text are taken from the Afghan history and are consequently authentic. So we gain an insight into the historical facts of Afghanistan over the years. Another aspect that can perfectly be used in class when working with the novel is the gender aspect in Muslim states like Afghanistan where women seem to be completely without rights. This also includes domestic violence when talking about Afghan women who miss almost all sorts of rights which is mirrored in the marriages of those women if we think of the polygamy in Afghanistan, for instance, which is quite common there. Apart from that one great aspect of the novel is certainly friendship as this is almost the only thing that makes it possible for Rasheed's two wives to bear all the violence and the cruel life they seem to be doomed to. These topics can all be treated in class and will certainly meet a positive response.

2.3 Summary of the novel

The novel "A Thousand Splendid Suns" by Khaled Hosseini is the second of his two novels at present. The author was born in 1965 in Kabul, Afghanistan. His parents were both working academics, his father being a diplomat and his mother a teacher of Farsi and history. The coup that took place in 1978 and the following invasion by the Russian military made the family flee for the United States where they received political asylum in the year 1980. They finally arrived in San Jose, California. His father started working there as a driving instructor. Khaled Hosseini works as a doctor and is living with his family, his wife and two children in Northern California. His first novel, The Kite

Runner, has received a very high critical but also popular acclaim.[5]

The novel is divided into four parts, the first concentrates on Mariam, one of the female protagonists in the story, whereas the second part brings Laila, the second female protagonist, into focus. As far as the third part is concerned, it portrays a mixture between
chapters about Mariam on the one hand and those about Laila on the other. The forth and
last part of the novel then is again concentrating on Laila. These two women are, as mentioned beforehand, the main protagonists of the story. They both live in Afghanistan, with Mariam born in 1959 while Laila was born in 1978, and although they have derived from totally different backgrounds, they will come together and develop a very intense relationship in the course of the story.

Mariam is a fourteen-year-old Afghan girl who lives with her mother Nana in a so-called kolba, which is a sort of shack. They live in Herat which is a rural area of Afghanistan. As she is an illegitimate child, she is not allowed to contact her father Jalil, to visit him or even to live with him. However, Jalil who is rich and has three wives with several own and legitimate children visits her every Thursday. Nana, in the meanwhile does not approve of his visits and so she always tries to convince her daughter about the fact that he does this only to silence his conscience and not because he has emotional feelings for his illegitimate daughter. On the day Mariam turns fifteen she plans to leave her mother's home in order to visit Jalil because he had promised to come but did not show up. Believing that she has lost her daughter forever her mother Nana commits suicide which she had in some kind announced to Mariam already before. As Mariam cannot stay in the kolba on her own she is brought to her father Jalil's house where his wives extremely disapprove of the thought of having the illegitimate child of their husband in their home. Consequently she soon must marry 45 year-old Rasheed, a shoemaker, who abuses her throughout their marriage, mainly for the reason that his wife Mariam is infertile. He once had a family, a wife and a son whom he had lost long ago which made him frustrated and pessimistic towards life in general.

The other protagonist of the story, Laila, lives in Mariam's neighborhood after the latter has been married to Rasheed for many years. Laila who is a beautiful young girl is a close friend of Tariq, a young boy who lives near Laila with his parents. After the war had begun in Afghanistan, Tariq's parents deny staying any longer in their home

[5]Hosseini, Khaled, *A Thousand Splendid Suns,* London: Bloomsbury, 2007. 415

town and so they leave the country. Unfortunately, Laila's parents get killed by a rocket as they were also attempting to leave Afghanistan. Laila's injuries make Rasheed and Mariam take care for her. After she has recovered Rasheed deceives Laila by telling her that Tariq is dead because she pleases him. This is why he really wants to marry her. As she is pregnant with Tariq's child she will not have any choice but marrying him. The child Laila gives birth to is a girl which makes Rasheed becoming abusive towards Laila, too. In the meantime Mariam and Laila become very close friends and make plans to escape from Rasheed. But

having failed only the first time, he deprives them of water for several days which almost kills Aziza, Laila's and Tariq's daughter. Years later Tariq appears outside the house. They are happy being reunited, but Rasheed hears of this as Laila let him in the house. His son Zalmai lets his father know about this. Furiously Rasheed starts to savagely beat Laila. Trying to help her Mariam kills Rasheed with a shovel. She confesses to the murder and will be executed, while Laila and Tariq leave for Pakistan with the two children Aziza and Zalmai, the latter being Rasheed's and Laila's son. The fall of the Taliban makes Laila and Tariq possible to return to Afghanistan. Together they fix up an orphanage where Laila starts working. She is pregnant with her third child which she will call Mariam.

3 Methodical Analysis

3.1 Portrayal of the procedure

The novel should be used for about twelve lessons at Realschule which will last circa three months. It is not worthwhile to extend this time span as this could probably result in students getting careless in reading the novel and working on it. In other words it could be superfluous for them to work that long on a text. In the given time span I would suggest among other things reading of some chapters together in class and also let the pupils read the chapters at home on a regular basis in order to be sure that they stick with the book. This is also why they should take notes about what they have read from time to time. The topics for each lesson should alternate and also the tasks that are required. All sorts of tasks should be included so students do not get the impression that reading is mundane but indispensable. With this mind I have compiled the following lesson plan for this novel.

3.2   Lesson Plan of lessons 1-12

1st lesson

In order to introduce the novel to be read the teacher introduces the book. He gives a short insight into the book by telling the pupils roughly what it is about, for instance where the story takes place. Having informed them about the content, he lets his pupils know who the author of the novel is, what his profession is, where he lives et cetera. Furthermore he can tell them about books the author has written apart from that novel. Getting started the pupils are to read chapters 1 and 2 which is pages 3 to 12 together in class. Afterwards the teacher lets the students guess further happenings that might take place after these two

chapters. They are to write down their ideas in their exercise books. The teacher finishes class by giving the homework which is reading the chapters 3 and 4, pages 13 to 24. Moreover they shall find a headline for the chapters 1 to 4 and write a short summary about they have read already.

2nd lesson

The lesson begins with the class reading together chapter 5, pages 25-36. The topics in these pages include belying one's promise, as Mariam has her birthday and is waiting desperately for her father Jalil who does not show up. The other topic Nana's suicide which follows Mariam's escape. The task for this lesson is to work in groups of 4 or 5 and answer the question: "Have you ever belied your promise or somebody you know did not keep his promise and why? Afterwards the students are to characterize Nana's reaction, i e. her decision to commit suicide. Students get transparencies to write down the answers. When finished, they are to present their results on the transparencies. Pupils should now talk about their results in a discussion which is led by the teacher. The lesson ends with the teacher announcing the homework which is as follows: Read the chapters 6 to 8, pages 37-

55 and write a short summary of the chapters.

3rd lesson

The third lesson begins with brainstorming about what has been read as homework, i. e. the chapters 6 to 8. These chapters contain the marriage of Rasheed and Mariam. The teacher writes the students' ideas on the blackboard. Afterwards the task is to write a dialogue about Mariam's and Rasheed's first conversation. Having finished the pupils present their results by reading out what they have written in the following way: two pupils, one male and one female take the role of Mariam and Rasheed. The lesson goes on with the reading

of chapters 9 and 10 together in class, pages 56-70. Finally the teacher informs the students about their homework which is reading the chapters 11 to 15, pages 71-103.

4th lesson

For this lesson the teacher wants to know if the students have all read the required pages and also if they have worked with the text. SO the teacher's task is to let the pupils take a written test on the content of the novel but only chapters 1 to 5. They are allowed to work with their partner if they want to but may also work on their own. They have roughly 20 to 25 minutes time. After the test the teacher goes through each question and shortly explains

what answer he had expected. Lastly he wants the students to read chapters 16 to 20, pages

107-142 for the next lesson.

5th lesson

The content of the pages the students had to read is about Laila, becoming the victim of bullying by other kids. The teacher wants to know whether they know how bullying can be defined and what, in their opinion, can be considered bullying among children. After this exchange of opinions the teacher forms groups of four who are to find answers to the questions "Did you ever experience bullying yourself or somebody you know?" and "How could bullying among children be reduced?" Their ideas are to be written down in short. The homework is to read chapters 21 to 26, pages 143-189.

6th and 7th lesson

These two lessons contain the topics war, as this is one aspect that is associated with Afghanistan , and the other one being teenage pregnancy. The teacher starts a discussion whereas he leads it. The questions being worked with are on the one hand "What opinions do you have of war?" and "Do you know any people who had to face war?" on the other hand. The students talk of their experiences respectively their knowledge about war. They shall think of possible ways to solve problems in the world without violence, i. e. war in the world. Aspects such as the necessity of war that is sometimes emphasized by some politicians should be included as far as possible. In groups of four or five they are to make notes about their thoughts and opinions. If there is time left, they change groups in order to also work with other peers. The task is to now brainstorm about the other topic, i. e. teenage pregnancy. Did any of the students experience it? This question is to be answered in group work. The question whether the state is able to intervene it shall also be talked about. This topic is to be continued in the seventh lesson. Two persons of each group present the results in font of the class. Next the teacher wants the pupils to write a personal comment about the topic "How would you have decided if you were Laila?" The background is that Laila, being a teenager has a sexual intercourse with Tariq the day he is about to leave Afghanistan with his parents. He urges her to come with him but she denies, refusing to leave her parents all alone in Afghanistan. She gets pregnant by this intercourse. So the students shall think of what they would have done if they were Laila. The students give their comments to the teacher at the end of the lesson. The homework is to read chapters 27 to 32, pages 193-228.

8th lesson

In this lesson the topic is that Rasheed marries Laila by deceiving her saying that Tariq is dead. Furthermore the first dialogue between Laila and Mariam who disapproves of the marriage takes place. Today's task for the students is to build groups of four or five and write a dialogue about Laila's and Mariam's first conversation after Rasheed tells her about the marriage. Each group presents its results on transparencies in front of the class. Lastly they discuss their results and at the end of the lesson, as usual, the teacher announces the homework which is reading chapters 33 to 36, pages 229-265.

9th and 10th lesson

These two lessons deal with the following issues: Laila stands up for Mariam when Rasheed is abusing the latter. The second issue is Laila's and Mariam's attempt to escape and their getting caught. The lesson starts with a discussion headed "Did someone ever stand up for you? In which way?" The pupils are to tell their opinions and experiences and afterwards they shall write down their experiences in short. The teacher collects the exercise books and corrects the texts of his students. The next step is group work which refers to the second issue. In groups of four the students are to work with the following question: "How could the story have been developed if the two women had been successful in escaping?" Their task is to prepare a role play which demonstrates the emotions of the two women. Having finished, they present their results whereas two of one group do the role play and the other two do some sort of stage direction. After the presentations the students get their homework which is to read chapters 37 to 45, pages 266-341.

11th lesson

This is the lesson that refers to the almost end of the novel. Tariq returns, Rasheed finds out about this and abuses Laila which results in the fact that Mariam murders Rasheed. The students shall work with their partner and find answers respectively opinions to the question "Would you denote the murder as poetic justice?" After the students have presented their results the teacher wants to read them the end of the novel at home which is chapters 46 to 51, pages 342-402.

12th lesson

In the last lesson with Hosseini's novel the topic is the plan made by Mariam. She confesses herself of having murdered her husband and is arrested consequently. Laila flees
with Tariq and starts a new life in Pakistan. Mariam is executed finally and the last thing that goes through her mind before leaving is "Legitimate end to a life with illegitimate beginnings" which refers to her life as an illegitimate child and its ending. Laila and Tariq marry, restore an orphanage in Pakistan and work there together. In this last lesson the students shall answer the question "What do you think of the novel's ending?" and afterwards they are to find another ending to the story. The task is to be done in groups of four or five. They present their results and discuss the following questions in class: "What is the significance of the novel's title?" and "Why do you think Hosseini chose it?"

3.3   Detailed Lesson Plan

Lesson Plan for one lesson (Lesson 2)

Phase	Content	Methods	Media
Warming up: 8.00 a.m. (~23 min.)	Reading of chapter 5, pages 25-36 together	Stimulus	
8.23 a.m. (~10 min.)	Pupils are given following questions: - Have you ever belied your promise or somebody you know did not keep his promise and why? - How would you characterize Nana's reaction? → Task: Work in groups of four or five and write down your ideas on a transparency	Group work	Transparency
8.33 a.m. (~7 min.)	Presentation of the results on a transparency		Overhead
8.40 a.m. (~3 min.)	Pupils are to talk about their results with the teacher leading the discussion	Discussion	
8.43 a.m. (~2 min.)	Homework for the next lesson: - Read the chapters 6-8, pages 37-55; - Write a summary about the given chapters		
8.45 a.m.	End of lesson		

4   Résumé

Taking into consideration the expectations concerning the suitability of a book in the English class it is obvious that this novel is useful for the purposes of tenth grade Realschule for it offers a wide range of pre- while- and post- reading activities as we have seen beforehand. The teacher has many possibilities to work with the novel in a reasonable way. Didactic methods such as group work, partner work, role play are just few of the various methods that can be used in class. As far as the content respectively the topics of the book are concerned it can be said that the novel opens up a kind of new world to the pupils who learn about the Afghan culture, its history and language to some extent but also about all the negative aspects that are connected with this country, e. g. the war which still is present today when we think of 9/11 and the current situation there. Moreover the position of women in this society which is allegedly stem from the fact of being a Muslim state is revealed impressively. In this case pupils can, for example find out for themselves if the treatment of women in Islamic states like Afghanistan really derive from being Islamic or if it is merely the abuse of the religion in order to fulfill their – the men's – own needs and desires. These prejudices can be wiped out by learning about the Islam by reading the Qur'an for example which will probably be a good way to broaden one's horizon in times of misunderstanding and ignorance among religions. In this case reading so-to-say leads to more reading which is certainly welcome. So we can emphasize that pupils can relate to authentic facts and happenings in the world and get the chance to see things from their own point of view and can interpret everything independent-minded. Apart from that, they learn how important it is to have friends, real friends who stand up for one in every situation of life, even if this means to make a sacrifice as it is in the case of Mariam. Of course this is an extreme example and pupils will in all probability never have such bad experiences but it makes them think about it. About aspects they have never imagined before, living in a democratic liberal state as Germany. To put it in a nutshell, the novel is suited for tenth grade, Realschule.

5   Conclusion

The question whether reading in the English class is unambiguously necessary can be answered in the affirmative if we sum up what is been said in the paper. Reading broadens one's horizon and helps pupils to elaborate information more effectively when using texts in class but also extracurricular. It makes them think in a sophisticated way and is a perfect way to learn further vocabulary as words are remembered more effectively when they are in context. If we look at the syllabus it is obvious that reading comprehension is highly recommended anyway. Either way it should be possible for pupils to read even more books than required, taking into consideration their own ideas. Every school should offer to every grade to read books that are not only meet the requirements of the syllabus but also interests of pupils in an extensive way. Books that broadens one's horizon and makes pupils look beyond the border of what they are used to. In this context I would highly recommend the given novel for there is also the authentic connection to real world conditions. It makes pupils aware of what happens in the world, it could deepen their sense for responsibility. When we think of the fact that Hosseini's readers asked for information about how Afghan women can be supported then young pupils will also b affected by his writings. As mentioned beforehand I would suggest it to be worked with in the tenth grade. To use it earlier would not be of great use as pupils younger than 16 are not mature enough to comprehend the message the book conveys. Taking everything into consideration I should emphasize the importance of reading at school and particularly in the English class.

6   Bibliography

Hosseini, Khaled: *A Thousand Splendid Suns,* London: Bloomsbury, 2007.

Internet sources
http://www.isb.bayern.de
http://download.bildung.hessen.de

Other sources
Fässler, Georg: Aufbaukurs Lektüre: *Reading.* Wintersemester 2010/11. Uni Erlangen-Nürnberg.